MW01268707

COMPLETE GUIDE ON HOW

TO PLAY THE HARMONICA

Harmonica Harmony: Unleashing the Soulful Sounds of the Blues in Your Hands(Teach Yourself to Play)

ISAK QUENTIN

Contents

CHAPTER ONE

INTRODUCTION TO THE HARMONICA

The harmonica has won the hearts of both musicians and music fans, from its simple start to its widespread use in many types of music. This book will talk about the harmonica's past, look at its different types, break it down into its parts, and give you tips on how to choose the best harmonica for beginners.

A Quick Look Back at the Harmonica

Early versions of the harp were made in China and Europe, which is where the instrument's roots can be found. But the harp as we know it today didn't really start to take shape until the early 1800s. A German clockmaker named Christian Friedrich Ludwig Buschmann is often given credit for creating the harmonica. He made an instrument called the "aura" that was similar to the harmonica but not quite as good. In the 20th century, the harmonica became very famous, especially in the US, where it was linked to blues music. Blues legends like Sonny Boy Williamson and Little Walter made the harmonica an important part of their bands, which influenced artists for many years to come. The harmonica has been used in many types of music over the years, from folk and country to rock and jazz.

NUMBER OF KINDS OF HARMONICAS

The Harp Comes In Different Types, And Each Has Its Own Strengths And Uses

The diatonic harmonica

This is the type that blues, folk, and rock songs most often use. Made to play in a certain key, which makes it useful for a wide range of musical situations. Only plays the notes in a single scale, but you can get to other notes by bending the strings.

Harmonica with Chromatics

It has a button on the side that lets players play all 12 notes of the chromatic scale.

Suitable for playing many types of music, such as jazz and classical.

More complicated than diatonic harmonicas; the player has to learn how to play notes that are triggered by buttons.

Harmonica with Tremolo

Each note has two holes, which makes the instrument vibrate when played.

It sounds a lot like a tremolo and is often used in folk music.

Harmonica for an orchestra

Harmonicas that are bigger than regular ones and made to be played in orchestras. This note is often found in film tunes and classical music.

THE HARMONICA'S PARTS

AND WHAT THEY DO

Harmonica players need to know about the harmonica's body because it affects how the instrument sounds. A standard diatonic harmonica is made up of a few main parts:

Comb

Harp's body, which is generally made of metal, plastic, or wood.

It has air passages that send air to the reed plates.

Plates with Reeds

Thin metal pieces with reeds put on them.

When air is blown or drawn through the harp, the sound is made by the reeds vibrating.

Reeds are

Sound is made by metal strips that move.

There are different notes because each reed is set to a different pitch.

Plate Covers

It has metal plates on the top and bottom.

Keep the reeds safe and shape the sound the instrument makes.

Parts of the comb

The player blows or draws air through holes in the comb to make different notes.

Labeled and numbered to show the musical scale.

HOW TO PICK THE RIGHT HARMONICA FOR NEW PLAYERS

If you are new to playing the harmonica, getting the right instrument is very important for a fun and good learning experience. When picking out a harmonica, think about the following:

Choose a Key

Figure out what key the harmonica is in based on the type of music you want to play.

Beginners often choose C major because it can be used in many situations.

Chromatic vs. Diatonic:

Since they are easier to play, diatonic harmonicas are a good place for beginners to start.

Chromatic harmonicas have more notes, but they might be harder for beginners to learn how to play.

QUALITY OF THE BUILD

Buy a harp from a well-known company to make sure it will last and be of good quality.

Good harmonicas sound better and respond better to different ways of playing.

Spending plan

There are high-end harmonicas on the market, but there are also a lot of great beginner choices that won't break the bank.

Try to find a harmonica that fits your wants right now and doesn't cost too much.

Tools for Learning

Think about harmonicas that come with easy-to-follow instructions.

For beginners, online groups and tutorials can also be very helpful.

The harmonica's past shows how popular it is and how well it fits into many types of music. Beginners who want to start making music with this movable and expressive instrument need to know about the different types, their parts, and how to choose the right harmonica. The harmonica is a beautiful instrument that can be played by people of all skill levels. Its melodies are perfect for fans of both blues and folk music.

CHAPTER TWO

THE HARMONICA UNVEILED: A COMPREHENSIVE GUIDE TO GETTING STARTED

INTRODUCTION

People can't get enough of the harmonica's soulful tunes and expressive tones. It's a small but powerful instrument. This guide will walk you through the most important steps to start playing the harmonica, whether you've never played before or want to get better. From the right way to hold your hands and stand to learning the shape of the harmonica and how to breathe properly to moving between single notes and chords, you'll go on a journey of harmony that goes beyond the limits of music.

HOW TO STAND AND PLACE YOUR HANDS CORRECTLY

Correct Placement of Hands

Getting your right hand in the right place is one of the most important parts of playing the harmonica. The hands work together to keep air out and keep the instrument under good control. This part will show you how to put your hands in the right places so that you can play notes that are clear and sound good.

FAQs

Q1: Why is it important to place your hands correctly when playing the harmonica?

A: Placing your hands correctly creates airtight seals that make it easier to control each note and stop extra air from leaking out, which leads to a clearer and more precise sound.

Q2: Can I improve the way I place my hands over time, or do I need to get it right from the start?

A: It's normal to get better at something over time, but starting out with a strong foundation and the right hand position will help you learn much faster and enjoy the game more overall.

Learning How The Harmonica Is Put Together

How a Harmonica Is Put Together

Before learning how to play, it's important to know how the harp is put together. This chapter breaks down the harmonica's parts, such as the reeds, chambers, and holes, and explains how they all work together to make the instrument's unique sound.

FAQs:

3. What are the reeds on a harp used for?

A: When you blow or draw air through the harmonica, the reeds vibrate, making different sounds. The harmonica's unique sound comes from putting these pitches together.

Q4: How can I tell the difference between the harmonica's holes?

Answer: Harmonicas have numbers on them that match the holes. Most of the time, hole 1 is on the left, and as you move to the right, the numbers get higher.

Breathing Techniques and Airflow: How to Get Good at Harmonica Breathing

When you play the harmonica, you need to breathe. This chapter talks about different ways to breathe, like diaphragmatic breathing and tongue blocking, which will help you make sounds that are steady and under control.

FAQs:

Q5: When I play the harp, should I focus on breathing in or out?

A: Drawing air in (inhalation) and blowing air out (exhalation) are both important parts of playing the harp. Finding a balance between the two will lead to a smooth and dynamic performance.

Q6: What is blocking your tongue, and how is it different from puckering?

A: To make chords, tongue blocking means filling several holes with your tongue. Puckering, on the other hand, means focusing on playing a single note through a single hole. Both methods have their own benefits and should be looked into.

What Are Single Notes and Chords?

Getting Around the Harmonica's Range

When you know the difference between playing single notes and chords, you can do a lot of different things. This chapter teaches you the skills you need to be able to describe individual notes and make chord progressions that sound good together.

FAQs:

Does it make more sense to start with single notes or chords for a beginner?

A: Starting with single notes will help you get better at being precise and in charge. As you get better, you can slowly discover the variety of chords.

Q8: How can I make the change from single notes to chords in a piece of music sound smooth?

A: It's important to practice and make small steps forward. Before putting them together, you should first understand each part on its own. Use easy tunes to work on smoothly switching between single notes and chords. When you start playing the harp, you need to be patient, dedicated, and eager to learn all of its different sounds. The information in this guide covers everything you need to know to start playing the harmonica, including how to hold your hands correctly, how to learn how to breathe properly, and how to move between single notes and chords. Whenever you play a note on the harmonica, know that you are getting better. Use the frequently asked questions (FAQs) and answers to figure out common problems, and don't be afraid to try new things to find your own voice in the peaceful world of this amazing instrument. Have fun playing.

CHAPTER THREE

BASIC PLAYING TECHNIQUES ON THE HARMONICA

With its small size and passionate sound, the harmonica lets players of all levels make a wide range of music. In this look at basic playing methods, we'll get into the basic skills that are needed to become an expert on the instrument. These methods will help harmonica players get better at everything from playing single notes accurately to using bends and overblows to make their playing more expressive.

1. Being very accurate when playing single notes

One of the hardest things for harp players to learn is how to play single notes that are clear and easy to hear. When you play chords, you have to play more than one hole at the same time. Playing single notes, on the other hand, takes accuracy and control. To get good at this basic skill, here are some tips:

METHOD OF THE PUCKER:

Cover one hole on the harmonica with your lips.

Concentrate the airflow on that hole and fill any holes next to it.

Try different lip positions and breath to get a clear, separate note.

Blocking the tongue:

If you don't want to go through certain holes, you can cover them with your mouth.

Move your tongue so that it only hits the hole you want to play.

Move your tongue around a lot so you can easily switch between holes.

Manage Your Breath:

Controlling your breath is important if you want to get regular breathing.Try holding your breath at different levels to find the best sound for each note.

To get better at keeping a steady beat while playing single notes, use a metronome.

2. How to Block Your Tongue and Pucker

Harmonica players use two different embouchure methods, tongue blocking and puckering, to get different tonal qualities.

Blocking the tongue

Cover several holes with your mouth, and use your tongue to block the holes you don't want to see.

To guide the airflow to a certain hole, make a seal around the holes.

For a strong, bluesy sound, this method is recommended. It is also necessary for techniques like octaves and splits.

Cracking up

Cover one hole or a group of holes next to each other with your lips.

Pay attention to getting the air to flow through the hole you picked.

It's easy to play different kinds of music with puffing, like tunes and clean single notes.

PUTTING TECHNIQUES TOGETHER:

Tongue blocking and puckering are two skills that skilled players often use together.

Try both methods until you find an embouchure that feels good and can be used in a variety of singing situations.

3. Overblows and bends for expressive play

For more skilled harmonica players, bends and overblowing add expression and feeling to their playing.

To bend

You can change the pitch of a note by changing the shape of your mouth.

Learn how to bend harp notes to get different pitches.

It's best to start with the lower holes because they bend more easily.

Too many blows

By blowing too hard, you can make notes that aren't naturally on the harp.

Needs very good breath and embouchure control.

Chromic sections are often played on diatonic harmonicas with overblows.

PLAYING WITH EXPRESSION

Use bends and overblows to give your playing more emotion.

Try bending your notes at different levels to add emotional depth to your music.

Add bends and overblows to scales and easy melodies as you practice.

4. The vibrato and other effects

To take your harp playing from simple to expressive, you might want to add vibrato and other embellishments to your repertoire.

A vibrato

Give notes that stay in tune a small pitch change.

You can get vibrato by changing the pressure of your breath or slightly moving the harp.

Try vibrato at different speeds and levels to get different sound effects.

Pull-offs and tongue slaps

By slapping the harmonica with your tongue, you can make percussion sounds.

For rapid effects, try pull-offs, which mean quickly taking your tongue off.

These tips will help you make your playing more lively and rhythmically interesting.

Sounds: trills

For a trilling sound, quickly switch between two notes that are next to each other.

To get faster, practice trills on different parts of the harp.

Trills can be used to make melodies sound better and make your music more exciting.

Moving parts

Try using different ways to articulate your speech, like slurring and tonguing.

Articulation gives your playing personality and helps you make each note sound clear.

Harmonica players who want to use the instrument's expressive potential must first learn basic playing techniques. Every skill a player learns, from playing single notes perfectly to using advanced methods like bends and overblows, helps them show feeling and musicality. Harmonica fans can start a rewarding journey of self-expression and creation through this fascinating and versatile instrument if they practice and learn more about it.

HOW TO PLAY THE HARMONICA IN DIFFERENT KEYS

Being able to play the harmonica in different keys is an important skill that lets you make a lot of different kinds of music. You can adapt to different styles, play along with other instruments, and add to your collection. We'll look at some useful tips in this guide to help you play the harmonica with confidence in a variety of keys.

1. Learning how to play the harmonica

Harmonicas are marked with a key that tells you what tone the instrument is. The C major scale can be played on a harp in the key of C, for instance. To play in tune with other artists, you need to know what key your harmonica is in.

2. Getting Harmonicas in Different Keys

If you want to play in different keys, you'll need harmonicas that are tuned to those keys. Start with harmonicas that are tuned to C, G, A, D, and E. Over time, you might want to add more unusual keys or keys that are widely used in certain types of music to your collection.

3. Getting to know the Circle of Fifths

The Circle of Fifths can help you figure out how different keys relate to each other. It sets up the keys so that you can see how close they are to each other and pick the right harmonica for the song. Move through the Circle of Fifths a lot to get used to how the keys relate to each other.

4. Getting better at transposition

When you transpose a song, you play it in a different key than the original. To get better at transposition on the harmonica.

Begin with a well-known song in a single key.

In the key it was written for, play it on your harp.

If you want to test yourself, play it in a different key using a harp in that key.

5. Getting good at playing positions

Harmonica players need to be able to play in a variety of situations. On a single harmonica, you can play a different tune in each position. First, second, third, fourth, fifth, and twelfth are the most usual spots. For instance, if you play a C harp in second position, you can play in the key of G.

6. Getting used to scale patterns

To play the harmonica well, learn how to play scale rhythms in different keys. Work on blues scales, pentatonic scales, major scales, and minor scales. This helps your muscles remember how to move and makes it easier to play the harmonica in different keys.

7. Trying out various methods

While you're learning new keys, try out different ways to play

Bends and Overblows

Learn how to do these things to get to more notes in different keys. You should try both tongue blocking and puckering to see which one works best in each key and style of music.

Vibrato and Articulation: Add expressive elements to your playing to improve how you understand music in different keys.

8. Using back tracks to play along

To get better at playing in different types of music, use backing tracks in different keys. You'll be able to adapt to different keys faster and better, and you'll sound better overall.

9. Learning How to Train Your Ears

Learn to tell the difference between different pitches and keys. Learn to play songs by ear, without using sheet music or tabs, by playing along with songs in different keys. This makes it easier for you to quickly find and play in different keys.

10. Recording your playing and listening to it again

Playing in different keys and styles? Record yourself. Critically listen to your records to find ways to make them better. This process helps you get better at what you're doing, makes sure you're accurate, and improves your total performance.

11. Joining groups that play the harmonica

Get involved with harp groups in your area or online. Talk about your experiences, ask questions, and get advice from people who know how to play in a lot of different keys. Help from other people can be very helpful on your harp journey.

12. Adding to Your Collection

As you get better at playing in different keys, learn songs from different styles to add to your collection. This variety makes you a more flexible harp player and lets you join in with a lot of different musical groups. Learning to play the harmonica in a lot of different keys takes time, practice, and a desire to learn new things. You can take your harmonica playing to new levels by learning the basics, improving your skills, and enjoying the variety of music that comes from playing in different keys. Being able to switch between keys smoothly will make you a flexible and skilled harmonica player, whether you're playing with other musicians, recording, or playing live.

CHAPTER FOUR

HARMONIOUS BEGINNINGS: LEARNING SIMPLE SONGS ON THE HARMONICA

Making your first steps into the world of harmonica playing fun when you start to understand how simple songs work. This guide will teach you the basics of how to play easy harmonica songs, whether you are a beginner with little or no musical experience or an experienced player who wants to improve their skills. You'll quickly become involved in the fun of making music with this small but expressive instrument as you learn how to read harmonica tabs, play melodies, add rhythm, and get the hang of timing.

An Introduction to Easy Harmonica Songs Unlocking the Potential of Music

The harmonica's appeal lies in how flexible it is; it can be used to play a lot of different songs. We will look at a variety of easy harp songs that are good for beginners in this chapter. This will make your entry into the world of music go smoothly.

FAQs:

Q1: If I've never played music before, can I learn how to play songs on the harmonica?

A: Of course! The harp is an easy-to-learn instrument that is great for people who are just starting to play. You can quickly learn to play your favorite songs if you work hard and practice.

To play the harp for the first time, what makes a song "easy"?

A: Songs for easy harmonica usually have simple tunes and use a small range of notes. They are made to help people who are just starting to play gain courage and learn important skills.

How to Read Harmonica Tabs

How to Read the Language of Music

Harmonica tabs are a way to see notes for music that is specific to the harmonica. This part will teach you the basics of reading harmonica tabs, which will help you learn songs and play them.

FAQs

Q3: What's the difference between normal musical notation and harmonica tabs?

A: Harmonica tabs are a simpler way to write music notation that is made for the harmonica. Tabs, not standard sheet music, show you which holes to play on the harmonica and how to do it.

Do I need to learn standard writing in order to play the harmonica?

Q: You don't have to know standard notation to play the harmonica. But knowing it can help. Tabs for the harmonica are a simple way to learn songs without having to learn standard musical notation.

PLAYING EASY MELODIES AND SONGS

Making songs come to life

You should be able to read tabs and play easy harp songs now. Next, you should learn how to play melodies. You can play simple tunes with ease after reading this chapter, which shows you how to turn musical notes into harmonica sounds.

FAQs:

How do I move from playing single notes to making a melody?

A: To begin, work on scales and easy patterns. Once you feel comfortable, play short tunes and make the rhythms more complicated over time.

Are there places online where I can find harp tabs for my favorite songs?

A: Of course! A lot of websites have a huge collection of harp tabs for many songs. Check out these sites to find tabs that fit your musical tastes and level of skill.

Adding rhythm and timing

Getting down with the harmonium

Timing and rhythm are important parts of musical performance. We'll talk about how to add rhythm to your harmonica playing in this chapter, which will make your shows more musical overall.

FAQs:

Q7: How can I get better at keeping time when I play the harmonica?

If you want to get good at time, use a metronome to practice. Start out with slower beats and slowly speed them up as you get used to them.

Question 8: Are there specific ways to add music to playing the harmonica?

A: Try tongue slapping, hand effects, and phrasing to add different rhythmic variations to your playing. You can get ideas and learn more about different rhythmic styles by listening to different harp players. When you start learning easy songs on the harmonica, you can play a lot of different kinds of music. Every note you play on the harmonica is a step toward learning this expressive instrument. Keep this in mind as you learn easy songs, read tabs, play melodies, and add rhythm and timing. Use the frequently asked questions (FAQs) and answers to figure out typical problems, get ideas from different types of music, and enjoy the process of making music with the harmonica. The harmonica has its own special charm that will take you on a melodic journey, whether you're playing for fun or to show other people. Have fun playing!

CHAPTER FIVE

INTERMEDIATE SKILLS AND TECHNIQUES FOR HARMONICA PLAYERS

As you learn to play the harmonica, starting to learn intermediate skills and techniques will let you make a lot more music. This guide will show you how to do everything from advanced bending and overblowing to learning different playing positions and exploring scales and creativity. It will be easy to understand and follow. We'll also talk about ways to improve speed and control, which are important skills for any harmonica player who wants to get better at singing.

The harmonica, which people sometimes call the "harp," is an interesting and versatile musical instrument with a long past.

FOLLOWING UP ON

BENDING

Learn how to bend the harmonica in deeper ways to take your skills to the next level.

As you get better at bending notes on higher holes, make it more tough.

Gain the control to bend notes correctly and smoothly, which will make your playing more expressive.

How to Get Overblows:

Play around with overblows to get to notes that aren't normally on the harmonica.

Start by blowing too hard into the bigger holes and work your way down to the smaller ones.

To get clear and controlled overblows, work on controlling your breath and embouchure very precisely.

PUTTING TECHNIQUES TOGETHER

For a fuller and more varied sound, add bends and overblowing to your playing.

Try mixing these methods in scales, melodies, and phrases you make up on the spot.

Learning these advanced methods will help you show more emotion and creativity.

Taking part in games from different spots

Getting to Know Positions

To improve your harmonic vocabulary, learn to play in different places.

In each place, a scale starts on a different hole on the harmonica.

Try playing in second, third, and higher places to see what sounds best with different types of music.

Getting Used to Positions

Learn what makes each role special and change how you play based on that.

For a varied and lively sound, use bending and overblowing methods in different positions.

When you play the harmonica in different places, you can get different sounds and use harmonica parts in more types of music.

A Starter Guide to Scales and Improvisation

To play scales on the harmonium,

On the harmonica, get to know the basic scales, like the major and minor notes.

To get better at playing the whole instrument, play scales in a variety of settings.

Knowing how to use scales is a good way to start improvising and being creative.

First Steps for Improvisation:

Play around with notes from the sounds you've learned to start learning how to improvise.

Begin by improvising simple phrases, and as you get better, add more complicated rhythms.

To get better at improvising, play along with backing tracks or get together with other players and jam.

EMBRACING YOUR CREATIVITY

When you improvise, you show who you are as a musician.

If you want to do improvisation, don't be afraid to try out different beats, dynamics, and phrases.

Accept mistakes as chances to find new ways to do things.

Getting better at speed and control

Using a metronome:

You can improve your speed and time by playing along with a metronome.

To get better, start at a reasonable speed and slowly speed up as you get better.

To get better at controlling your guitar, play scales, arpeggios, and licks at different speeds.

Clear Speech and Articulation

Pay attention to making each note sound clear, even when you're playing faster.

Learn how to pucker and block your tongue to get better at playing precisely.

Learn how to use legato and staccato phrases to make your music more interesting.

Control that changes

Learn dynamic control by getting good at changing the volume and strength of your sound.

Playing softly and loudly can help you show different feelings through your music.

Dynamic control makes it easier to show how you feel and keep people's attention.Getting to the level of intermediate harp skills and techniques is a fun step that lets you explore more types of music. As you get better at bending and overblowing, try out different playing positions, learn scales and improvise, and work on getting faster and more controlled, remember that the most important things are to be patient and keep practicing. Enjoy the thrill of discovery, and let your harmonica playing change as you get better at it and find your own musical style.

CHAPTER SIX

STYLES AND GENRES IN HARMONICA PLAYING

The harp is a flexible instrument that can be used in many types of music, each of which provides a unique opportunity for expression. This look at styles and types will include the things that make blues, folk, rock, jazz, and other styles unique. Key things that will help you on your harmonica journey are learning how to play in different ways, studying famous harmonica players, and getting tips on how to play with other musicians.

TRYING OUT DIFFERENT TYPES OF MUSIC

Harmonica for blues

The harp and blues go hand in hand; the instrument has been very important in the development of the style.

For true blues harmonica playing, you need to learn how to bend the notes.

To show the emotional depth of blues music, use expressive word choice and lively singing.

THE FOLK HARMONIUM

Folk music, which includes both old and new folk styles, gives harp players a lot of different things to play.

Pay attention to playing melodically and clearly, and try out different playing positions to fit the form of folk songs.

Folk music with harmonicas often makes you think of stories and old times.

The rock harmonium

Indelible marks have been left on rock music by famous harmonica players who played on many great rock songs.

Try playing with an amp and trying out techniques like overblows to get that strong sound that is associated with rock.

The rock harmonica can play anything from fast, distorted melodies to smooth background music.

THE JAZZ HARMONIUM

Jazz is a difficult and advanced style for harmonica players to work with.

To play the complicated chord progressions in jazz, you often need to know how to play the chromatic harp.

To get the feel of jazz, work on improvising and learning the subtleties of jazz technique.

HARMONICA FOR COUNTRY AND BLUEGRASS MUSIC

The harmonica is an important part of both country and bluegrass music, adding to their lively and twangy sounds.

Focus on playing clearly and cleanly, and try tongue blocking techniques to give your music a unique country sound.

In country and bluegrass music, the harmonica often goes well with banjos, fiddles, and guitars in upbeat and lively songs.

Changing the way you play the harmonium to fit different styles

Techniques that are flexible

Learn a variety of techniques that you can use to meet the needs of different types of music.

Try out different ways to play, embouchure, and articulate to find the best fit for the style you're using.

HOW LOUD AND HOW SOFT

You should change the way you play to fit the tone and volume of each type.

For blues, you might need a rough, emotional tone, but for jazz, you might want a smoother, more controlled one.

Try using hand and cupping methods to change the tone and get different stylistic results.

Listening and Taking It In:

Listen to a lot of each type of music to get to know its subtleties.

Listen to harp players who have made important contributions to each style and look at how they play.

Learn the subtleties of each style so that they can influence how you play.

LOOKING AT IMPORTANT HARMONICA PLAYERS

Blues Stars

Learn more about the blues harp greats Sonny Boy Williamson, Little Walter, and Junior Wells.

Look at how they bend the notes, how they use emotional language, and how they use amplification.

Blues harp players often use call-and-response patterns, so pay attention to how they play with other instruments.

Pioneers of rock

Get into the early rock harp styles of John Popper of Blues Traveler or Mick Jagger of The Rolling Stones.

Look at how they use effects, loudness, and incorporating their music into rock arrangements.

Rock harmonica can play anything from slow, soulful songs to fast, distorted solos.

The Jazz Masters

Learn more about the harp music of Toots Thielemans and Howard Levy.

Pay attention to how well they play the chromatic harp and how well they can play through tricky jazz progressions.

It's important to pay attention to how these players flow through chord changes when they play jazz harmonica.

Virtuosos in Country and Bluegrass

Harpists like Charlie McCoy and Jelly Roll Johnson can help you learn about country and bluegrass music.

Look at how they block their tongues, speak clearly, and fit into the lively sounds of these styles.

You should work on your speed and agility because country and bluegrass harp playing is often fast-paced and melodic.

ADVICE ON HOW TO JOIN A BAND OR PLAY WITH OTHER MUSICIANS

How to Listen and Blend

Pay attention to the other instruments in the band to figure out what your part is in the whole.

Harmonica is often used as a background or lead instrument, so change how you play to fit in with the rest of the group.

Talking and moving around

Talk to other musicians during practice and concerts to make sure that your music makes sense.

When you play, know when to be soft and when to step forward with a strong solo.

Experimenting and Working Together

Be willing to try new things and work with other artists.

Jam sessions are great places to try out new styles, ideas, and harmonica skills in a friendly setting.

Thoughts on Gear

Pick out the harmonica and amplifier that are best for the song.

Talk to the band about the effects and amplification settings to make sure the sound is balanced.

Learn the Repertoire

Learn all of the songs that the band plays and how the harmonica fits into each one. You should change the way you play depending on what the piece calls for.

Finally, moving between styles and types on the harmonica is an exciting adventure that lets you hear a lot of different kinds of music. It's fun to play the harmonica in different styles, whether you're interested in the raw emotion of blues, the storytelling nature of folk, the energy of rock, the sophistication of jazz, or the lively spirit of country and bluegrass. Learn from the greats, try out different techniques, and be open to working with others to create your own unique harmonica style and add to the rich web of musical expression.

THE END

Made in United States
Troutdale, OR
03/15/2024